Beginning the Courts of Heaven (Pocket Size)

Beginning the Courts of Heaven (Pocket Size)

UNDERSTANDING THE BASICS

Bill Vincent

RWG Publishing

CONTENTS

RWG Publishing

PO Box 596

Litchfield, IL 62056

https://rwgpublishing.com/

Published in the United States of America

1

∾

Beginning the Courts
of Heaven

I want to give you some information that will actually help you be a success and move to where God wants you to go. When Jesus taught on prayer, he touched on prayer throughout the Gospels, and you would find this in Matthew and Mark, for instance, there are illustrations or ideas concepts concerning prayer, in other words, you would see him praying all night long. Or you would see him getting up very early in the morning and praying in the book of John. You see principles of prayer being spoken of, but in the book of Luke, in particular, you see Jesus teaching on prayer and painting pictures of prayer. So, we would kind of understand what was going on in the spirit realm when we prayed. And let me just say one of the main things that shifted for me when I began to understand the courts of Heaven; it was my concept of the Spirit realm, and I'll clarify this then move through here. I used to think that the spirit realm was about a battlefield, but I discovered that the spirit realm is actually about a courtroom you see in the spirit realm.

We are in a conflict when we pray. But here's the issue because that conflict you see in the conflict of a battlefield and the conflict of a courtroom are two separate things. And if I am actually in, I'll prove this to you if I'm actually in a courtroom, but I think I'm on a battlefield and I could be using the wrong protocol. Just try to get things accomplished and to get things done. Have you been praying prayers for a long time and haven't seen an answer? Let me tell you why that has happened so often, and we think well I must be doing something wrong, I must be displeasing to God. Maybe I don't have enough faith, then we start blaming it all on ourselves, or maybe it's not the timing of

God, and this is the problem I have because we think well it's not the timing of God while everything's falling to pieces. Marriages are being destroyed, financial ruin is happening, people are dying prematurely, and yet it's not the timing of God. I think that's a crazy idea that all these evil, even irreversible things are happening. But the reason they are happening is that it's not the time of God to answer my prayer. Let me give you one other idea of what it might be. It could be that it has nothing to do with the timing of God. It could be that something legal is resisting you in the spirit realm. That something legal is stopping God from being able to answer your prayers.

To help you understand all this, we need to talk about dimensions in Luke eleven and Luke 18 when Jesus began to teach about prayer. You see the disciples came to Jesus in Luke eleven verse one and two, and this is what they when said they saw him; they said Lord teach us how to pray because they were watching him praying and Jesus said in response to that when you pray, say our father which art in heaven hallowed be your name. The Lord's Prayer the motto prayer whatever realm we want to call it, but Jesus said this that the first dimension of prayer is approaching God as Father. You see the first round. Jesus taught them about was approaching God, his Father. Well, here's the problem you also need to understand as so many believers do not have a concept of God His Father. And if they do, it's a wrong concept because of some past illustration of a father that they might have had. So, the issue is that only by the Holy Spirit, Paul calls him in Romans 8:15, the spirit of adoption and only by the spirit of adoption can we know him as Father. It's then that the spirit of adoption comes into our hearts, and he calls us to cry out Abba Father remember that. So often do we emphasize the Abba side, but we forget the father. Paul was not repeating himself when he said the spirit would cry out Abba Father. He was saying the fatherhood of God has two aspects. It has the Abba side which is loving endearing, always accepting will never reject you, will heal you, and will do all the things we desire and need to be done because we all have to know him as Abba, but he also has the side of Father Abba Father. So, in the fatherhood of God, not only is there the endearing side of his fatherhood watch this, but there is also the authority's side of his fatherhood. See

Abba is the endearing side, Father is the authority side. We have to know God in both dimensions. Abba Father both the endearing, loving, accepting, not rejecting anyone but also as a father that will discipline. He set us for our own good so that we can become our protectors of his holiness. That's what the Bible says. So, when the apostle Paul says the spirit of adoption comes, he is going to release to us both aspects of the fatherhood of God. Now, why am I saying this? Because Jesus said, the first dimension of prayer in Luke eleven is to approach God as Father. So whenever I am approaching him I am approaching him as Abba Father the One who loves me unconditionally but the one who will also prepare me for my future and the destiny that he has for me because anything else as a father would be irresponsible because he loves me enough to prepare me and to correct me when I need to be corrected. He helps me in dealing with issues that need to be dealt with, whether it is in my marriage or in raising my children or in my character or whatever it may have been. God says I am going to work in you my very nature so that now you can not only reflect me, but you also know me not just as Abba and not just as a father but as Abba Father.

Can I give you a little secret here? If all I know him is as Abba. That's going to lead to lawlessness because it is all accepting and loving my flesh. I'm sure maybe yours doesn't, but my flesh will tend to take advantage of that. Does your mind? I need to know him like that, but I need that aspect of who he is. But you got to understand that that's all I know of him. Then I'm going to become lawless in my nature and lawless in my activities. Now watch if all I know of him as is father, the one that has the authority, then I'm going to become legalistic.

Because I'm trying my best to please him because he's the one that has the authority, and guess what? Lawlessness and legalism both lead to the same place, and it's called darkness, so God says I'm going to come, and I'm by my spirit going to reveal to you. Abba Father, the one that is the all accepting one but the one that will also prepare you for the destiny and the future that is beyond your comprehension and what he has for you. So Jesus said when you approach God, the first dimension is you approach him as father, and I want to say this; I believe that we have to be so firmly established in approaching him as Father because that is the basis for every other thing we do. I believe that with every fiber of my being that I have to approach him as Father God. As the loving Heavenly Father, as the above Father, that will break and reveal Himself to me so that I can approach him in those matters. That's the first dimension. Well, we've spent a whole lot of time. That's the first dimension. When you pray, say Our Father, who hath in heaven.

Then he continues in Luke eleven and verses five through eight; he starts unveiling another way that we approach God or the second dimension in prayer he said which of you have a friend that would come to him at midnight. And he said of his friend coming at midnight, and he said, You know I need something for my journey. And you don't have anything to help him with. You would get up, and you would go to another friend, and you would say to this other friend please get out of bed and give me what I need so I can help my other friends come on this journey he said even though this friend will not get up and give you what you're asking but because he's your friend he'll get up and give you what you're asking. This is my version because then you leave him alone, and he can go back to sleep. That's the basis of the parable. So, the point is that all of a sudden, Jesus shift gears, he says in his teaching that the first dimension is approaching God his Father. That's the basis of all praying and all relationships with God. But the second dimension is approaching him as a friend, and this is different.

You see, we can know him as Father but not know him as a friend. See what makes him our friend, Jesus said John 15 said I no longer call you servants. I call you friends because everything the father tells me I'm telling you. So, friends are those. That God can share his secrets with seeing the father. With kids, there are things I don't tell them. I don't know about you. I mean as I grow maybe, but even then, it's like I don't know if they can handle this. But my friend I can trust with secrets because that's what Jesus said a friend was one that he could tell things so that he wouldn't tell anybody else. Why is this why being this important. Well, we don't have to look any further than Abraham. Abraham was called the friend of God at least three times in Scripture. And what did God do? Whenever God comes down, and he sees the condition of Sodom and Gomorrah, he says I'm going to have to destroy it. Its evilness demands my justice. It's evil.

This demands it be destroyed because the cry of it comes before God, and God says this I cannot do this without telling Abraham. Now, why did you want to tell Abraham?

Well because he is his friend, but God also knew this that Abraham, as his friend would understand why God was telling him. God's telling me as his friend what he's going to do because he wants me to seek to give him a reason not to. Why. What's one bad side as God is always looking for a reason to be merciful. You have to get that and quit condemning what God's not condemning. You will quit judging what God's not judging. Jesus said you condemn the guiltless because you don't understand it is our mercy and not sacrifice. So, God tells Abraham for one reason because he knows that Abraham as his friend will know his heart. And he'll know why he's telling him now. The Bible never told us that he knew why he was telling him, or God didn't tell him that. But Abraham, as the friend of God, knew the heart of God, knew the secrets of God.

So, as God told Abraham, he is telling me because he wants me to do something about it now, I don't know how many times in my life where I have known things on a national level in America, and I would ask why he is telling me this. Why do I see this? Why do I know this? Because I have no platform to do anything with this. Then I found this, and I thought this was why he was telling me he wanted me to step before him as his friend and seek to give him the reason for this not to happen.

We are called to be God's friend. I thank God for us getting our personal needs met, but God has a governmental place in the spirit realm that he wants us to occupy that can literally shift things concerning nations of the earth. Hebrews twelve twenty-three says we have come to a church, the firstborn Church of the Firstborn that's registered or recognized in heaven. This house has a rank in heaven. Not just as individuals. This house (the Church) has a rank in heaven that gives it the right to deal with issues not only concerning the United States but concerning nations of the earth if we know how to move into this realm. Because that's exactly what Abraham was doing, he was dealing with an issue concerning a region, concerning an area of the earth. Are you getting this?

Galatians 2 and verse 5. He says, for though I am absent in the flesh, Paul said, yet I am with you in the spirit now. Paul does not just say now. Now guys, I just love you so much. I'm with you, know when he says I'm with you in the spirit, it means he's there looking in the spirit. You'll find this also in first Corinthians five when they were not dealing with the scene that's in the church and Paul saying the same thing there that they need to deal with this thing because he's looking in the spirit at where they are and what they're doing and not doing. Though I am absent in this flesh, I'm with you in the spirit rejoicing to see your good order and the steadfastness of your faith in Christ. He said I am looking at you in the spirit, and I see your rank in the spirit. In other words, I'm seeing the jurisdiction God has given you that you need to take that jurisdiction and not just be a blessed people but literally as God's friend be able to deal with issues that can change the course of nations. That's what Abraham was seeking to do as God's friend. What do you do?

God is saying I don't need the whole lot to repent I need my government; I need my church to take its place before me. Our assignment is to be his friend. God says, upon this rock, I will build my church... Matthew 16 18. Here's what it means.

We say called out once, but when you understand the culture in which you were speaking, it was the atmosphere that set in the city gates making decisions concerning a city or a region. So, as the called-out ones for governmental purpose, God says I'm looking for my church my government to take its place before me as my friend and give me the right I'm looking for. To be able to shift things in nations so that the will of the kingdom begins to occur in nations and not what the enemy wants. See, I believe we're here to change nations from the spirit realm. As his friend, I could go on to talk to you about the Council of God, but that's not there. That's what we're doing in this book, but this is the second dimension. We approach him as Father and Jesus. First, learn how to approach him as a father and a revelation of who he is. Secondly, learn how to approach him as a friend because he talked about a friend going to a friend to get something for a friend. I'll get back to that. Okay. So, he teaches those two dimensions of prayer. Luke 18 let's just say for the sake of argument that the disciples are practicing these two dimensions, Jesus tells them about to approach God, his Father, approach him as friend, approach him as Father this is the way I pray and I want you to learn how to do these two dimensions or two rounds of prayer. Jesus said there in Luke 18 verse 1 and Jesus spoke this parable that men ought always to pray and not to lose heart. So his purpose for this next teaching is not to be a child cheerleader to unlock a mystery, an additional mystery about prayer that's going to get answers the other two rounds didn't get because when Jesus says he's saying this to you so that you will pray and not give up. *He's not being a cheerleader he's loosing*, I'm about to give you a secret that's helps to get prayers answered that have not got answered up to this point. The other two dimensions are great, but any prayers you're not having answered is because there is a third dimension. I want to bring you into this, so then he says this, there was a certain a widow in a city who went before an unjust judge and said to the unjust judge avenge me my adversary and he wouldn't for a while, why wouldn't he? Because he's unjust. He doesn't render verdicts based on justice; he renders verdicts based on what you'll give, a bribe, a promotion whatever the situation may be. But the has nothing; she has no influence, she has no money, she has nothing to bribe the judge with so he won't give her anything because he's not interested in justice, he's interested in just padding his pocket, but the problem was that this widow kept coming back. Every time the judge turned around, she was back on his docket. Because that's where you approach judges in his courtroom, you're not knocking older daughter home, you're appealing to them in a judicial system, so this judge finally says I will give her what she wants because she's saying avenge me of my adversary, get justice for me. The judge said I'm going to give her what she wants less by her continual coming she weary me out much as Jesus said here what the unjust judge said and shall not God avenge his own elect that cries out to him day and night. Yes, I say he will reward them speedily so what's he saying? He's saying if you've been praying a long time if you learn how to come into the judicial system those prayers you've been praying a long time, the answer can come speedily. Why? Because something legal is resisting you. That one hasn't work by approaching God his Father, what hasn't even worked by approaching him, his friend all of a sudden there's a third dimension, a prayer of knowing how to approach God as a judge. Watch this step into the judicial system of heaven. Because judges' rule over judicial systems and see things shift legally in the spirit so that now the prayers you've been praying can be answered.

So, let me back up just a little bit in these three dimensions. I just want to make this point to you really quickly in these three dimensions when we play by the way in the judicial system. The moral of that story is not that God's an unjust judge, but you have to convince him. We know that's not true. It's this that if this widow could get a verdict from an unjust judge, how much more can we come before the righteous judge? The God of all the universe, the judge of all the universe, and have him render verdicts on our behalf because we are his elect. That's the moral of the story. If she could do it in a hostile situation how much more will it work for those of us that are his elect? That's the whole moral of the story. So, let me give you these three things. Jesus when he was teaching about approaching his father, he then talks about this, that a father gives bread, fish, and eggs to their children. So here's the issue when I approach God for my own needs, for my own stuff I am appealing to his fatherhood, my fish, my eggs, my bread, my needs, my wants, my provision, whatever it may be on whatever level I'm appealing to his fatherhood. So, when we approach God as Father, it's almost always about our own stuff. Because guess what fathers do, they meet needs. I'm a father of three. I'm still meeting needs. I will tell the mom; I will tell this lady I'm not doing that anymore. And then they'll come, and they'll ask me, and I start trying to figure out how to do it again because something stirs in my father's heart when they ask me for stuff. Fathers meet needs; our Heavenly Father meets our needs; we appeal to him for our needs, which is what happens as a friend in addition to everything else I said. Watch what's happening here is that a friend that has a friend come to him, he can't help him, he doesn't have the sufficiency to help. So, what does he do? He goes to another friend, notices this friend is in the middle that's a position of intercession. So, what's he doing. He's appealing to this friend to meet the need of another friend. So, I approach God as Father for my own needs; I approach him as a friend for the needs of others. This is a position of intercession, and that's what Abraham did. That's what Moses did. Those are the friends of God they always appeal to God for the needs of others; it's a position of intercession that God wants to move us into even for nations. But watch this, we approach him as Father for our own needs. We approach him as a friend for the needs of others.

We approach him as Judge, hear all he's about to say when we're dealing with an adversary because this is what the widow was doing; avenge me of my adversary. Now we're going to get to the core of what I want to say, avenge me of my adversary. And when you say there's in every picture that Jesus painted about prayer he never put pressure on the battlefield, but he did put it into a courtroom, this amazed me I know that there are battlefields that Paul talks about in different things but Jesus the one teaching on prayer never put picture prayer on a battlefield. He always pictured it in a courtroom in Revelation 19:11, the Bible says that when Jesus comes back on the white horse with the armies of heaven with him. Here's what it says, it says he will come back to judge which is judicial activity and then to make war. Here's the point. You never go to war against your adversary until you first been to court. If you tried to go to war against your adversary before you've been to court, you will be backlashed against, and I'll prove this to you. The enemy can only do what he does if he's found the legal right to do it. I've just given you some of the reasons why your life has been in such a mess, especially the inner sensors. Because we've been binding demons that have a legal right to operate, and you can't bind them until the legal right is taken away. So, you have to learn how to do this improper protocol in order of the spirit. And this is what pulls it. I am looking at your order in the spirit, there's an order in the spirit that we need to make sure we're walking in accordance with so that we are functionally operating from the rank and the position that God wants us to operate from. Is that making sense to you? Watch what I'm about to say, the word adversary in Luke 18; avenge me of my adversary in the Greek word; it means one who brings a lawsuit. That's what the word means. It's a legal position in the spirit realm. He's the first Peter five-eight be sober be vigilant for your adversary. The same word causes the devil. So, it tells us who we're talking about; we're naive at the devil who is occupying a legal position and has the right to bring lawsuits. This is the Apostle Peter. So, don't tell me this isn't new testament. All this is going to happen in the New Testament. Peter said you got to be sober you got to be vigilant make sure you're not giving him any right to build a case against you legally because your adversary that is called the devil walks about like a roaring lion seeking whom he may devour. In other words, he cannot devour at will. He has to discover a legal right to do so. If he could devour it, we'd all be dead. But he can't... he can only devour what he has found a legal right. He's the one that he's the goes down... goes means one who brings a lawsuit, it comes from two words and time and because that's really deep and time means to deny. So, the purpose of the lawsuit is to deny you what's rightfully yours. This is why you've been praying prayers for years that are in agreement with God's word, and yet there's been no answer because he has a legal right to deny you what's rightfully yours. He has a case against you in the spirit realm that you will never deal with by approaching God, his Father. You will never deal with it approaching God as a friend, and will have to deal with it by going before him as a Judge is stepping into the judicial system of heaven and un-doing the case that's against you at the moment, it is undone. The answer comes speedily.

So, we have to learn this third dimension father's great friend is God. But listen, going before the judge will get answers that we haven't gotten yet. You say how'd you learn this. I know desperation. In my own heartache, out of our own heartaches, we had situations we couldn't stop. It was getting worse. We were late. We were doing everything we need to do. We were living the way we knew to live, and yet our lives with our children and us, and our finances and reputation and everything were falling to pieces, and the scary part was not even how bad it was. It was that we couldn't stop it. I didn't want to and the phone or go to the door. Or even turn on the computer because it was something else coming at us. I was worried I was doing everything I knew to do. I couldn't stop it.

Then the Lord graciously began to teach me about the courts of heaven, and I will go into some of this. Because the legal right the enemy was using. So, somebody can come in I don't believe that would go far. This is what I always tell people if what you're doing is working, just keep doing that. But if it's not working, you might check this out because it brought an unprecedented break-through for us. I mean situation after situation began to come into divine order. When we began to deal with the courts that even know that stuff, then we had a legal right to bring a case.

Now let me just give you one more scripture because that's Peter that said this. Revelation 12 verse 10, it says that there is an accuser that is accusing us before God; accusing the brethren before God day and night. We overcame him; they said they overcame him by the blood of the lamb. The words of her testimony love not life to death. Yes, that did happen at the cross. I believe in the finished works on the cross because I, we go into the courts on the basis of his finished works. But here's what it says, there is an accuser who is in the great court categories. But guess what it means a complainant in a judicial system a complainant at law. This is another picture of what's going on in this third dimension. But here's what I want you to see if you're thinking, you ought to be thinking, wait a minute how does satan build a case against me? What's the legal thing he's using that's stopping God from answering my prayers, what's happening here? Because he says we're not to give him the legal rights, we're to be sober, vigilant, so what are the legal things that can be used against us to build a case against us?

There are three basic things that can be used against us. There could be many more, but we're not going to go there right now. They can literally all be consolidated in these three. Paul assuming David in Psalms 32 and Psalms 51 spoke of three distinct words when he was dealing with righteousness before God; he spoke of sin, transgression, and iniquity, and he uses the same three words in Psalms 32 and Psalms 51. Sin means to miss the mark in both the Hebrew and the Greek. It also has to do with motive, a motive is very important because, in *Job 1 and 2*, the accuser brought a case against Job on the basis of Job motives, see what God says to him when he's in the courtroom. Have you considered my servant Job, or do you have a case against him? And he said he only serves you because you put a hedge about him take the hedge away, he won't serve you. So, what was he doing? He was saying Job's motives for serving you are wrong. God could tell you why he had the right to do that, but we will go there. The bottom line is that the accusation against Job was the motive and intent of his heart. So, what does that mean?

That means that we are not supposed just to do the right things. We're supposed to do the right things for the right reasons. Let me just tell you why he could accuse him. Why could he accuse him based on motives?

In the courts of heaven, I don't have time to go here in the courts of heaven. Your offering has a testimony attached to it. You can find that Hebrews 7 verse 8, His offering given from a wrong heart allowed the enemy the right to accuse him of wrong motives. That was enough for him to be thrown into tribulation. So, what do we need to do? Malachi. Chapter 3, he comes to purify our hearts that we might bring an offering in righteousness. We have to let him purify our hearts so that our offerings are with the right motives. Why am I bringing this offering? Because I love you. Because I love you, you're your great, you're glorious, you're awesome, and I loved you with all of my beings. I'm not trying to manipulate you. I may actually be practicing sowing and reaping. But that's different than manipulating. Our offering has a sound attached to it. So, motives are very important. Very important. I've literally had to pray and cut off past offerings from people. Saying Lord, don't let them see, that's something some people like. I gave an offering, and things got worse. I know I just baited you right there. I know what I did.

He said the word was in the second word, transgression; transgression means to stride or to step across a line. It speaks of activity against God. So, whereas sin can be more about motive and intent and enmity of the heart, transgression is about activity now. Now here's the deal we all know our stuff. Well, here's what I tell people we need to follow the admonition repent quickly. Why? Because you have a demon, who's looking for a legal right to devour. So what I do I try to abide by first John chapter two, little children I write these things to you that you not sin but if you say when you have an advocate with the father Jesus Christ the righteous and he's standing on our behalf, and I can go into the courts of heaven, and I can say, "Lord I repent, and I'm asking for the blood to speak for me please. The blood that speaks better things. I'm asking for the blood to speak and the mediator of the new covenant, which is you yourself to speak for me and all the voices I'm asking for these things to be done. So, we deal with our own issues. The third thing is the word iniquity, and this is the main one. See and is about intent transgression, which is about activity iniquity in the sin in the bloodline. And you know people say well that's not right I've heard all sorts of people try to explain all sorts of things away, so it's not really a generational curse, it is generational addictions or generational habits. If it's working against me and my family line, the bottom line is it still operates; you may say well how does it work? Because this iniquity that's in the bloodline was what the word iniquity meant, it's not just about my personal sin per se as it is about that which is in the bloodline now iniquity is for basic things.

Number one it gives the enemy a legal right to tempt you in a given area. Almost all strongholds come from an iniquitous route. Almost all. Iniquity gives the enemy a legal right to attempt in a given area. Number two iniquity will fashion your identity and the way you think about yourself if you let it. Isaiah Chapter 6 says what was me. I'm undone. Now he's in the glory of God woe is me I'm undone. He literally means I'm so wicked I should be destroyed whenever his iniquity is purged with a call from all at the altar. He then says when he hears God talking watch in ensuring his spiritual senses were awakened, the moment is iniquity was dealt with; he could hear more clearly watch what else happens he says here am I. When he hears the Lord, who will go for us who can we sin. He said here I am sending me to all of a sudden; he went from one that was worthy to be destroyed to one that was worthy to be a prophet of God. See what happened iniquity purged iniquity and dealt with, will fashion your identity, number three iniquity not dealt with will detour you from your destiny in it. I'm finished with this iniquity and dealt with it, would detour you from your destiny see Psalms 139 sixteen says that before you existed in the earth, you were a scroll or a book in heaven. So, it says as my days yet unfashioned and my substance yet unformed, they were written in a book of Heaven about me. So before I existed in the earth as a human being, there was a book about me in heaven, so you have to get this, on the day you were born, you weren't just a sweet little baby that came into the earth, you were a scroll that landed out of heaven. But here's the problem you landed in a body connected to a bloodline. And the enemy used the iniquity of your bloodline that that body is connected to, to try to pull you off course for what you were originally meant to accomplish. I ask you how many people living under bridges today that are homeless because of alcoholism, drug addictions, mental illness, whatever were destined, and written in their book they were supposed to cure cancer. Or come up with some other major breakthrough. But the enemy used the iniquity in their bloodline to pull them off course from what their real intention was out of heaven. Because the enemy will use the iniquity in the bloodline to pull us away from the destiny we were meant for could tell you stories but don't have time. No, for the last one, I'll get to you iniquity is used by the enemy to build cases against you in the courts of heaven. In 2nd Samuel Chapter 21, there's been a famine in the land for three years.

David is the king and the king for a long time. Listen because of that broken covenant; it has given the enemy a legal right to now bring a famine into the land for three years, and if you want me to answer your prayers for the land you're going to have to go back into the history of Israel and deal with the broken covenant. That Saul committed by breaking the covenant will give you a night. So, David goes. And finds out the Covenant. I figured it out as to give me that's what he needs to do. Does it and the Bible make an astounding statement, it says, and God heeded the prayer for the land? Watch all the prayers have been prayed for three years, and suddenly when the legal issue that was stopping the prayer from being answered was dealt with then, the prayer was immediately answered. Please hear me. You have to know how to undo the legal case against you. If you want God to answer your prayers because if you have been praying prayers for a long time and there's been no answer is because something legal is standing in your way. I live this way. I think this way now, if I ever hit resistance or there is no answer, or God shows me something that the enemy wants to do, I know he can't do it without a legal right and be finished with this.

There is an altar; there's a sacrifice, and wherever there's a sacrifice or something is speaking that's opening portals. And the reason some people are under depression is that there's a demonic portal open over them and their bloodline. We're going to really get him free. We got to shut that portal. We've repented for all this, and now I want you to make this statement. I want you to say, *"Lord, not only am I repented of the blood that has been shed, and I know that I now,* say Lord let the alter that has been caused to be in place, be torn down. Now Lord, let us sacrifice on that altar so, it does not speak anymore and let the portal that has been opened, let it be shocked the moment we do that. Everything changes in the atmosphere. God wants to set some people free. Would you say, Hey, I got some issues one way or the other with depression?

Thank you, Father. For being my Abba father. That loves me. That meets my needs; I thank you for that revelation. As my father, thank you that you're my friend that you share your secrets with me. And then more and more, you're willing to un-veil your secrets so that we can shift things, even in the realms of the spirit. We thank you for that, but we also want to thank you that you are in charge. Thank you, Lord, that when Jesus died on the cross. That was the greatest legal. Transaction of history and I am coming before you as Judge based on that transaction.

Then I can come before you. Buy the blood and the body of Jesus that has made me righteous. So, I come to stand before you in your righteousness. But Lord, any case that the accuser has against my family and me, I want to come, and I wanted to repent. I ask that any sin. Any pure harm motive, any wrong motive connected to all friends, I repent of my work to bring an offering in righteousness. So, I am asking that any offering that has been out of a wrong motive in the courts of heaven so that it cannot be used to build cases against my family or me, I say Lord let my motive be pure. Let me love you and be loved by you. Lord, I also repent for any and every transgression. Every act of rebellion against you, from my heart or inactivity, I repent I asked for the blood to cleanse me. I asked for every bit of shame connected to that to be removed by the blood. Lord, I asked you to cleanse me right now in Jesus' name. Not just before a year before the Lord. Anything concerning motives is considered concerning transgressions, evil or bringing something to mind, just specifically tell the Lord I repent of this, and I asked for the blood to speak for me before your courts and every accusation to be annulled and to be silenced because the enemy has no answer for the blind. Thank you, Lord, for just doing this right now in the name of Jesus.

LET THE LIBERTY OF GOD NOW COME. THAT THE LIBERTY OF GOD NOW COME.

THAT THE LIBERTY OF GOD NOW COME.
NOW!

About the Author

Bill Vincent is no stranger to understanding the power of God. Not only has he spent over twenty years as a Minister with a strong prophetic anointing, but he is now also an Apostle and Author with Revival Waves of Glory Ministries in Litchfield, IL. Along with his wife, Tabitha, he leads a team providing apostolic oversight in all aspects of ministry, including service, personal ministry, and Godly character.

Bill offers a wide range of writings and teachings from deliverance to experiencing presence of God and developing Apostolic cutting edge Church structure. Drawing on the power of the Holy Spirit through years of experience in Revival, Spiritual Sensitivity, and deliverance ministry, Bill now focuses mainly on pursuing the Presence of God and breaking the power of the devil off of people's lives.

His books 50 and counting has since helped many people to overcome the spirits and curses of Satan. For more information or to keep up with Bill's latest releases, please visit www.re-vivalwavesofgloryministries.com. To contact Bill, feel free to follow him on twitter @revival-waves.

Signs and Wonders Revelations
Children Stories
The Rapture
The Secret Place of God's Power
Building a Prototype Church
Breakthrough of Spiritual Strongholds
Glory: Revival Presence of God
Overcoming the Power of Lust
Glory: Kingdom Presence of God
Transitioning to the Prototype Church
The Stronghold of Jezebel
Healing After Divorce
A Closer Relationship With God
Cover Up and Save Yourself
Desperate for God's Presence
The War for Spiritual Battles
Spiritual Leadership
Global Warning
Millions of Churches
Destroying the Jezebel Spirit
Awakening of Miracles
Deception and Consequences Revealed
Are You a Follower of Christ
Don't Let the Enemy Steal from You!
A Godly Shaking
The Unsearchable Riches of Christ

Heaven's Court System
Satan's Open Doors
Armed for Battle
The Wrestler
Spiritual Warfare: Complete Collection
Growing In the Prophetic
Faith
The Angry Fighter's Story
Understanding Heaven's Court System
Restoration of the Soul
Spiritual Warfare Made Simple
Aligning With God's Promises
Deep Hunger

Web Site:
www.revivalwavesofgloryministries.com